Reading for Every Child
Comprehension

Grade 1

by
Karen Breitbart

Published by Instructional Fair
an imprint of
Frank Schaffer Publications®

Instructional Fair

Author: Karen Breitbart
Editor: Kim Bradford
Interior Designer: Lori Kibbey

Frank Schaffer Publications®

Instructional Fair is an imprint of Frank Schaffer Publications.

Send all inquiries to:
Frank Schaffer Publications
8720 Orion Place
Columbus, Ohio 43240-2111

Reading for Every Child: Comprehension—grade 1

ISBN: 0-7424-2811-7

4 5 6 7 8 9 10 PAT 11 10 09

Table of Contents

There are thirteen different types of pages for each of the six main comprehension strategies in this book. The pages may be copied and used in a number of different ways.
- Group them by strategy, and use them as a whole class, in small groups, with the Title 1 teacher, reading specialists, tutors, or after-school programs.
- Copy, laminate, and use in centers.
- Copy onto transparencies and use for whole-class activities.
- Use the pages and activities as "Comprehension Strategy Units" with your students.
- Display finished products and have an Open House, featuring student work.
- At the end of a unit, set up a "Comprehension Strategy Museum," with one room per strategy. Invite parents and other students. Completed *Book Projects* make nice features.

Use this table to help you find pages that will meet your needs.

Page Type	Page Description/ Suggestions	Main Idea and Details	Story Structure	Sequence	Prediction	Conclusions	Cause and Effect
		Comprehension Skills listed by page number					
Teacher's Resource	Find an introduction to and ideas for each skill.	6	19	32	44	56	68
Graphic Organizers	Use in any subject throughout the day when you want to highlight the way a reading comprehension strategy can help students understand material.	7	20	33	45	57	69
Introduction and Direct Practice	Use to introduce or remediate each skill as part of a packet, a pullout lesson, or whole-group work.	8	21	34	46	58	70
Writing Prompts	May be copied, laminated, and cut apart to use in a center, on a ring, or in a box as cards. They may also be copied on transparencies and used on the overhead.	9	22	35	47	59	71
Writing Activity	Work on the comprehension skill during writing workshop.	10	23	35	47	59	71
Math	Apply comprehension strategies to math problems.	11	24	36	48	60	72
Social Studies	Use as part of social studies lesson, homework, or packet.	12	25	37	49	61	73
Science	Use with science class, as homework, centers, or packets.	13	26	38	50	62	74
Fine Arts	Partner with art or music teachers to expand on these ideas.	14	27	39	51	63	75
Read-Aloud/Listening	Use to teach strategies through modeling any time you read for listening comprehension.	15	28	40	52	64	76
Book Project	Assign and display as creative book reports.	16	29	41	53	65	77
Reading Take-Home Record	Use as nightly book homework that practices a specific comprehension strategy. Model how to fill them out in class, at open house, or at conferences; student reads and fills out; listener signs.	17	30	42	54	66	78
Games	Play during transitions or down times and use in centers.	18	31	43	55	67	79

Reading First

The Reading First program is part of the *No Child Left Behind Act*. This program is based on research by the National Reading Panel that identifies five key areas for early reading instruction—phonemic awareness, phonics, fluency, vocabulary, and comprehension.

Phonemic Awareness

Phonemic awareness focuses on a child's understanding of letter sounds and the ability to manipulate those sounds. Listening is a crucial component, as the emphasis at this level is on sounds that are heard and differentiated in each word the child hears.

Phonics

After students recognize sounds that make up words, they must then connect those sounds to *written* text. An important part of phonics instruction is systematic encounters with letters and letter combinations.

Fluency

Fluent readers are able to recognize words quickly. They are able to read aloud with expression and do not stumble over words. The goal of fluency is to read more smoothly and with *comprehension*.

Vocabulary

In order to understand what they read, students must first have a solid base of vocabulary words. As students increase their vocabulary knowledge, they also increase their comprehension and fluency.

Comprehension

Comprehension is "putting it all together" to understand what has been read. With both fiction and nonfiction texts, students become active readers as they learn to use specific comprehension strategies before, during, and after reading.

Introduction

The goal of reading instruction is to produce good readers who enjoy reading. A good reader not only reads the words in the text correctly, but also makes meaning from the text. Good readers have personal interactions with the author by relating the text to his or her own personal experiences. Making meaning and relating personal experiences are essential parts of reading comprehension. Reading comprehension is one of the hardest things to teach because there are so many components involved. This book breaks down the different skills used by good readers. It contains activities which can be used to lay the foundation necessary to build the following comprehension skills: finding the main idea, recognizing story structure, sequencing, predicting, drawing conclusions, and recognizing the relationship between cause and effect.

Reading comprehension strategies can be taught and learned before children can actually read. They can be used when the children are listening to stories that are being read out loud. Using these strategies while listening to text helps lay the foundation necessary for future success in reading comprehension.

Reading comprehension skills can be practiced all day long. This book is designed to help facilitate lessons or activities that introduce or lay a foundation for comprehension strategies. Each section contains an introduction to the comprehension skill as well as graphic organizers, a skill worksheet, journal prompts, a writing activity, listening comprehension activities, a reading record sheet, a game, and activities to be used during math, science, social studies, and fine arts. All of these activities are open-ended and can be used as a supplement to any unit or prescribed curriculum.

With the help of these activities, teachers will find sneaky ways to introduce reading comprehension skills throughout the day!

Teachers: The following pages will assist you in providing your class with many opportunities to practice finding the main idea in a paragraph or a story. Being able to find the main idea will strengthen your children's ability to comprehend or "get the meaning" out of print.

Helpful Tips:

Explain that "main idea" is simply the main reason that the author wrote the story or paragraph. For example, have the children complete the following sentence:

The main reason you eat lunch is… (because you are hungry, to give you energy, to keep you healthy).

Write the children's responses on the board. Lead the class in a discussion about their responses and help them choose the best response.

Ask the class if "because you like peanut butter sandwiches," "because your Mom gave you a cookie for dessert," or "because we go to lunch at 11:30" are good responses. Tell the children that these responses do not tell the *main reason* for eating lunch. Explain that these ideas are the *details* that tell

about someone's lunch.
The activities found on the following pages will help strengthen the reader's ability to find the main idea in stories and paragraphs as well as find details that help explain the main idea.

Share with parents:
• A Friendly Letter (p. 10)
• The Daily News (p. 12)
• What Did I Learn in Science? (p. 13)
• Advertise Your Book! (p. 16)

Additional pages to reinforce main idea and details:
• Writing Activity: This Is How (p. 35)
• Learn a Lesson While Reading (p. 65)

Answer Key
Page 8
1. Coins
2. a
3. Answers will vary.
4. • Some sell lemonade.
   • others help with yard work.
   • children can wash cars, sell cookies, or walk dogs.

Page 11
Story Problem #1
• Answer – Eight bears went to the picnic.
• Main Idea – Bears were going to a picnic.
Story Problem #2
• Answer – Six girls were in the club.
• Main Idea – The girls like to jump rope. The girls had fun jumping rope.

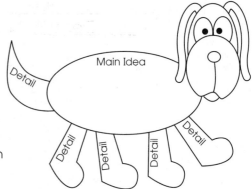

◎ Comprehension

Organize Main Ideas and Details

Directions: Use these to help you with main ideas and details.
Think about what you read. Write the main idea in an organizer.
Then write the supporting details.

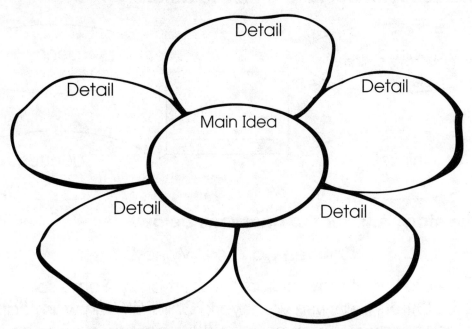

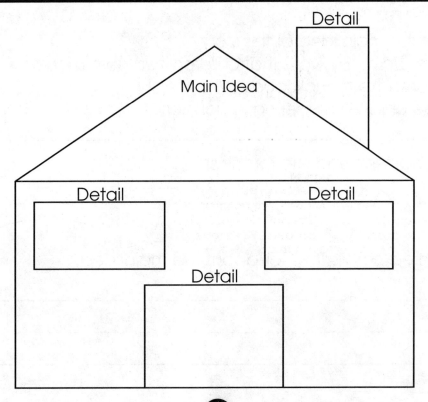

Practice Main Ideas and Details

A **main idea** is what the writing is mostly about. **Details** tell more about the main idea.

Write the correct main idea for these details.

1.

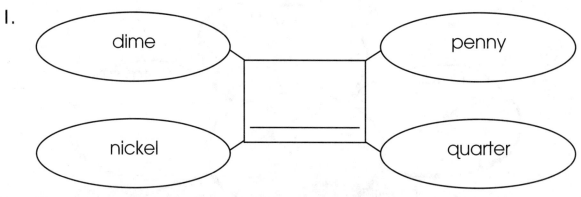

dime   penny   _____   nickel   quarter

Read the story. Answer the questions below.

Children Can Earn Money

There are lots of ways children earn money. Some sell lemonade. Others help with yard work. Children can wash cars, sell cookies, or walk dogs. Many children think earning money is fun.

2. What is the main idea of this story?
   a. There are many ways that children can earn money.
   b. Children like to walk dogs.
   c. Some children like selling lemonade.

3. Write another good title for this story.

_____

4. Write three details that tell about the main idea:

   • _____

   • _____

   • _____

Teachers: Practice main idea and detail skills with these journal prompts. Enlarge and cut them into cards for centers, use them on the overhead, or make a journal-prompt die.* Choose a prompt as the main idea. Students can write it in their journals with supporting details.

Journal Prompts

Main Idea	Main Idea	Main Idea
This weekend, I had a lot of fun.	_____ is my favorite sport.	Birthday parties are exciting.
Main Idea	**Main Idea**	**Main Idea**
Exercise helps make you healthy.	If I could get a new pet, I would get a _____.	My best friend and I have fun together.

*To make a die

1. Cut

2. Tape

3. Fold and tape

Extra Journal Prompts

It is important to eat a healthy lunch.

My mom is a great mother.

There are many reasons that my favorite color is _____.

I do chores at home to help my family.

A Friendly Letter

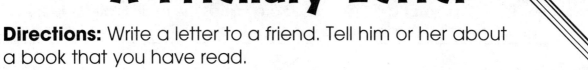

Directions: Write a letter to a friend. Tell him or her about a book that you have read.

Dear _____ ,

I just read a good book. It is called

The main idea of the book is

My favorite part of the book is when

You may want to read this book for yourself!

Your friend,

⊚ Comprehension

Teachers: Have students work together to act out the following math story problems. After acting out the story problem, the class can work together to solve the problem and tell what the main idea of the story is. Answers can be found on page 6.

OPTIONAL: Have the children make up their own math story problems.

Act It Out!

Story Problem #1

There were 5 bears walking through the woods on the way to a picnic. When they got to the middle of the woods, they saw 3 more bears.

"Would you like to go to a picnic with us?" the bears asked.

"We would love to," the other bears answered.

How many bears went to the picnic?

Story Problem #2

Three girls were playing jump rope. They were having a lot of fun.

"I love to jump rope!" yelled one of the girls.

"Me, too!" called out another girl.

Three other girls were across the street watching all of the fun. They decided to join in and jump rope, too.

"We can start a club called 'The Girls Who Love to Jump Rope'!" said one of the new girls.

"Yes, let's all be in the club," answered another girl.

How many girls were in the club?

Teachers: Have children prepare news reports to present to the class. After each news report is presented, the class can tell what the main idea is and discuss what details help to support the main idea.

The Daily News

Preparation:
- Find a large empty box. Cut a large rectangle hole in the bottom of the box. This will be the screen. Fold in the sides of the box. Use markers to draw an on/off button and volume control. Use the cardboard left over from the cutout to make a remote control.
- Assign each child a day to present his or her news report.
- Make one copy of the bottom of this paper for each child to take home. This will help the children prepare their news reports.

Name_____

The Daily News

I will be the newscaster on _____. Please help me prepare my news report. Thank you!

The main idea of my news report will be:

_____

_____

These are details that will help tell about my main idea.

1. _____

2. _____

3. _____

What Did I Learn in Science?

Directions: Complete this page to show main ideas and details you learned in science.

I am learning about

_____

These are
some things
I learned.

◎ Comprehension

A Musical Story

Teacher's Note: Look for a song that tells an appropriate story and is easy for the children to understand. Children's music, country music and folk music often tell a story.

Directions: Listen to the song several times. Let the song tell you a story. Answer the following questions.

The **main idea** of the song is: _____

_____

What **details** in the song tell about the main idea?

• _____

• _____

• _____

What do you think the song would look like if it were a picture? Draw it here.

_____

14

Teachers: Use this activity to reinforce main idea/detail skills during read-aloud time.

Incoming Beanbags!

Materials: three red beanbags and one blue beanbag

Activity:

1. Read a paragraph or page of a book to the children.

2. Throw the beanbags to some of the children.

3. The child who catches the blue beanbag will tell the main idea of what you just read.

4. The children who catch the red beanbags will recall one of the details that support the main idea.

5. Continue reading, periodically stopping to throw the beanbags and ask for main ideas and details until the story or reading selection is complete.

Ideas for books that illustrate main idea and details:

Amazing Spiders by Alexandra Parsons

Discovering Butterflies by Douglas Florian

Dolphin by Robert A. Morris

The First Dinosaurs by Dougal Dixon

The Jurassic Dinosaurs by Dougal Dixon

The Last Dinosaurs by Dougal Dixon

Seeds by Terry Jennings

Advertise Your Book!

Directions: Choose one of your favorite books. Make a
TV commercial that will make others want to read it, too!

1. Write or draw pictures in the spaces below. Put the main idea
   in the center of the circle. Put the details inside the squares.
   They can be four interesting things that happened in the story.

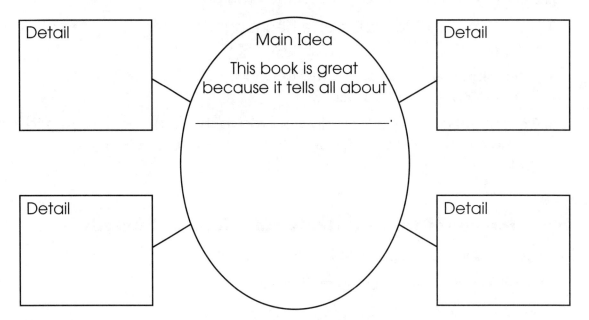

Detail

Detail

Main Idea

This book is great
because it tells all about
_____.

Detail

Detail

2. Use this information to make a television commercial! Act out
   your commercial for a friend or to the class. Have fun!

   • First, show your book. Read the title
     and author.

   • Next, read or tell the main idea.

   • Then, read or tell the details.

   • Last, tell people why they should read
     the book.

 **Comprehension**

Teachers: Enlarge and send one of these slips home with nightly books to reinforce main idea/detail skills.

Name _____ Date _____

Title and author _____

Pages _____ Signature _____

In the spaces below, write one main idea with three details from your book.

Main Idea

Detail Detail Detail Detail

Name _____ Date _____

Title and author _____

Pages _____ Signature _____

In the spaces below, write one main idea with three details from your book.

Detail

Detail Detail

Main Idea

Teachers: Have fun practicing main idea/detail skills with this game.

What's the Main Idea?

Type: a game to help the children practice figuring out main ideas from a given set of details

Set up: Copy the game cards and cut them apart.

Procedures: The object of this game is to guess the main idea by listening to details. Divide the class into teams. Draw one card. Read the details. The first team to guess the main idea will earn a point. The team with the most points wins. Answers are upside down on each card. You may leave them as is, fold them over, or cut them off.

#1 • Dogs like to play chase. • Dogs like to play catch. • Dogs like to do tricks.  Main idea – Dogs are fun.	**#3** • Apples are crunchy. • Grapes are sweet. • Oranges are very juicy. Main idea – Fruits are tasty.	**#5** • Put on a coat. • Put on mittens. • Put on a hat.  Main idea – We dress warmly on a winter day.
#2 • At school, we learn about math. • At school, we learn to read. • At school, we learn about science.  Main idea – We learn at school.	**#4** • Brush your teeth. • Wash your face. • Put on your pajamas.  Main idea – Get ready for bed.	**#6** • Get a towel. • Put on a bathing suit. • Put on sunscreen.  Main idea – Let's get ready to swim.

Optional: After the children have used these cards, divide them into groups and have them make up their own cards by writing three details that tell about a main idea. Use their cards to play another round of "What's the Main Idea?"

Teachers: The following pages will help you focus students on the key elements in a story. When students approach a story with a mental framework of expectations, they are more likely to catch and retain what is read, leading to improved comprehension.

Helpful Tips:

Story structure refers to the main parts of a story. These are the unwritten "rules" for writing a good story. Stories from centuries ago and from across the world all address the same story structure. Story structure refers to the following:
- Characters
- Setting
- Plot
  - What is the problem?*
  - What events occur to solve the problem?*
  - What is the outcome of the problem?*

*These are parts of the plot.

Understanding story structure helps children strengthen their comprehension in several important ways. For one, they know what to look for while reading. This focused approach leads to greater recall and an improved ability to retell the story.

Understanding story structure also aids children in writing better stories. Children can use their knowledge of story structure to create a "story map" that can help organize their thoughts before a writing assignment. This will help them produce a more complete story.

Share with parents:
- Dioramas (p. 29)

Additional pages to reinforce story structure:
- Drawing Conclusions from Art (p. 63)

Answer Key

Page 21
1. Jamie
2. a
3. • put away her doll
   • made her bed
   • hung up her clothes
4. Jamie had fun playing.
5. Jamie's house.

Page 26
Main characters – the class
Setting – outside
Problem – We want to learn about chemical changes.
Events – They measured the baking soda, added vinegar, and observed the fizzing and bubbles.
Solution – They learned that a chemical change has taken place when there is fizzing and bubbles. They saw a chemical reaction firsthand.

⊚ Comprehension

Organize Story Structure

Directions: Use these to help you organize important parts of a story. Think about what you read. Then write down the story elements in one of the organizers.

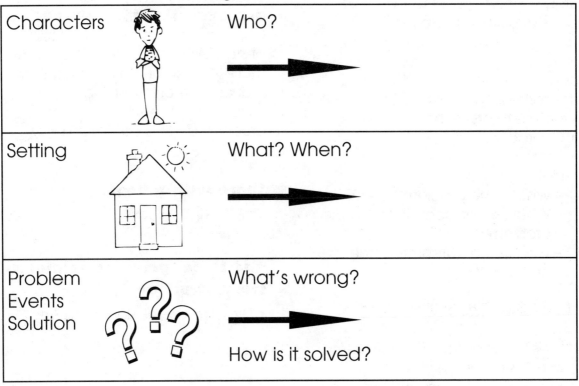

Characters		Who? →
Setting		What? When? →
Problem Events Solution		What's wrong? → How is it solved?

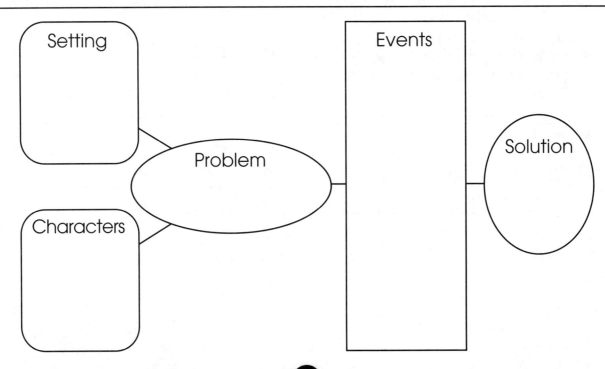

Setting

Characters

Problem

Events

Solution

0-7424-2811-7 *Reading for Every Child: Comprehension*

◎ Comprehension

Practice Story Structure

Story structure is the way a story is organized. The **story elements** are *characters*, *setting*, and *plot* (*problem, events, solution*). They help you understand a story.

Directions: Read the story. Then answer the questions.

Jamie's Problem

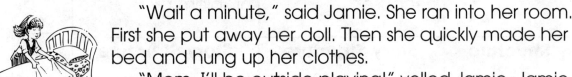

Jamie's friend rang her doorbell.
"Can you play?" asked her friend.
Jamie's mom said she had to clean up her room first.
    "Wait a minute," said Jamie. She ran into her room. First she put away her doll. Then she quickly made her bed and hung up her clothes.
    "Mom, I'll be outside playing!" yelled Jamie. Jamie and her friend had fun playing all afternoon.

1. Who is the main character? _____

2. What was Jamie's problem?
    a. She had to clean her room before she could play.
    b. She made her bed.
    c. She had a lot of fun playing with her friend.

3. Write three things Jamie did to solve her problem:

    • _____

    • _____

    • _____

4. How did the story end? _____

5. Where is the setting in this story? _____
    Draw the setting below.

Comprehension

Teachers: Practice story structure skills with these journal prompts as students write about important elements in their favorite stories. Enlarge and cut the prompts into cards for centers, use them on the overhead, or make a journal-prompt die.*

Journal Prompts

Story Structure	Story Structure	Story Structure
Character: I did not like the main character in the book called _____ because …	**Setting:** My favorite book is _____. It takes place in _____. I would like to visit here because …	**Plot:** My favorite character had a problem. _____'s problem was _____. _____ solved this problem by …
Story Structure	**Story Structure**	**Story Structure**
Character: I like to read stories with main characters that are animals because …	**Setting:** I think _____ is the perfect setting for a story because …	**Plot:** I like to read stories that have happy endings because …

*To make a die

1. Cut

2. Tape

3. Fold and tape

Extra Journal Prompts

Character: My favorite main character is _____. I would like to be friends with this character because …

Plot: The main problem in the story called *Goldilocks and the Three Bears* was _____. One way to make sure that this never happens again is to …

Setting: If I were going to write a story, I would make it take place in the time of _____. I think this would be a good time period for a story because …

Plot: If I were going to write a story about a cat, I would make the problem be _____. I would have the cat solve this problem by …

22

If I Had Been There...

Directions: Pretend that you are one of the characters in your story. What would you do if you could change the story? Write about it.

Title: _____

Hello, I am _____. If I could

do things differently, I would _____

_____

_____

_____ .

Here is a picture of how things will turn out next time:

Math Story Problems

Directions: Use story elements to make up your own story problem.

Example:

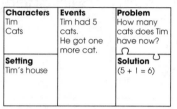

Characters Tim Cats	Events Tim had 5 cats. He got one more cat.	Problem How many cats does Tim have now?
Setting Tim's house		Solution (5 + 1 = 6)

Tim had 5 cats. Then 1 more cat came to his house. How many cats does Tim have now?

1. Plan your math story problem here:

Characters	Events	Problem
Setting		Solution

2. Write your math story problem here:

_____

_____

_____

_____

_____

3. Trade with a friend and solve each other's story problems!

Comprehension

Current Events Story

Teacher's Note: For this activity, look for a story about a local person that is uplifting and touches on all of the story elements.

Directions: Listen to your teacher read something from the local section of the newspaper. Think about the story elements and fill in this story map with words and pictures.

Current Events Story Map

This is the main character in the story:_____	The setting was: Where? _____ When? _____

The problem was _____
_____

These are some events that were mentioned:

1. _____
   _____

2. _____
   _____

The ending was_____ (happy or sad).

Teachers: Writing a class story about your science experiments is a good way to practice reading comprehension skills in science. This may be done with any experiment. Below is a sample experiment with a chemical change, which makes for exciting plot events! (This activity is a good outside activity. It is messy!)

Story Element Science

Sample Experiment: Cool Chemical Change

Materials: two Dixie cups and a plastic teaspoon for each small group of children, vinegar, and baking soda

Activity:

1. Tell the children that a *chemical change* takes place when you mix items together and something different is created. This new material will be totally different from the original things mixed together. Also tell the children that when a chemical change has taken place, you can sometimes feel a temperature change, see a color change, see gas produced (you will see and hear fizz), or see a solid created out of liquids.

2. Show the children the materials for the experiment. Ask the children to make predictions about what will happen when you mix all of the ingredients together. Write their predictions on the board or on chart paper.

3. Take the children outside. Give each group two cups and one plastic spoon. Have them perform the experiment as follows:

   - Put three spoons of baking soda into one of the cups.
   - Next, fill the second cup with vinegar.
   - When you say, "Cool Chemical Change!" students should pour the vinegar into the cup with the baking soda.
   - The children will observe as the baking soda and vinegar react by producing a gas. (This is the bubbles and the fizzing sound.)

4. Remind the children that this is an example of a chemical reaction because a gas is formed. Have them share their thoughts about the chemical change that made the liquid bubble over.

5. Bring the children back into the classroom and have them help you write a story about what they did. Help them include all of the story elements. Start the story with the sentence, "Today our class wanted to learn about a chemical change."

6. After writing the story, read it to the children. Have the children find the main characters, the setting, and the plot (including the problem, the events, and the solution). Answers are on page 18.

⊙ **Comprehension**

Poetry and Story Structure

Teacher's Note: Shel Silverstein, Judith Viorst, and Jack Prelutsky are popular poets with children.

Directions: *Story structure* can be found in poetry. Choose a poem and read it. Then fill in the story map below. Draw a picture for the poem.

Characters: _____

_____

_____

Setting: _____

_____

_____

The problem was _____

_____

Fill in the title and author. Then draw your picture here. Show the **characters** in the **setting** acting out the **problem**.

Poem Title: _____

Author: _____

Comprehension

Teachers: Use this activity to reinforce story structure skills during read-aloud time.

Beach Ball Blast!

Materials: two large blow-up beach balls and a permanent marker

Preparation: Use the permanent marker to write one of the following in each colored section on the beach balls:
- Who is the main character?
- Was the main character good or bad?
- Do you like the main character? Why or why not?
- When did the story take place?
- Where did the story take place?
- Tell about one of the events.
- What was your favorite part?
- How did the main character solve his or her problem?
- What happened at the beginning of the story?
- What happened in the middle of the story?
- How did the story end?
- Did you like the way the story ended? Why or why not?
- What would you have done if you were the main character?

Activity:
1. Read any story, poem, or nonfiction reading selection.
2. Toss the beach balls to two of the children listening. Have each child read aloud and answer the question that is showing on the top of the beach ball when it is caught. Collect both balls.
3. Continue reading and tossing the balls until the end of the story. This will increase your children's attention and listening comprehension.

Ideas for books that illustrate story structure:

Alexander and the Wind-up Mouse by Leo Lionni

The Best Dressed Bear by Mary Blocksma

The Bremen Town Musicians by Hans Wilhelm

Corduroy by Don Freeman

Dirt Boy by Erik Jon Slangerup

The Library by Sarah Stewart

Moongame by Frank Asch

Teachers: Making dioramas will help the children focus on the different elements present in stories.

Dioramas

Materials: index cards, various art materials, and one shoebox for each child in the class

Activity:

1. Choose a story for the children to work with. Read the story to the class and then have the children re-read it.

2. Make a big story map with the class, listing all the important story elements: characters, setting, problem, events, and solution. Assign each story part to a student or group of students. (You can plan it so there are enough events for the rest of your students or groups.)

3. Pass out an index card to each student or group. Have them copy their assigned parts onto the cards. (For example, "Characters: three pigs and a big, bad wolf," or "Event 1: The three pigs build their own houses.")

4. Pass out the shoeboxes and let students tape their index cards on the top (which is technically one of the long sides that will be on top when the diorama is complete).

Tape card on top

5. Allow children class time to work on their dioramas, or assign them as homework. When they are done, line up all the boxes this way: characters, setting, problem, events (in order), solution. Have children take turns presenting their part of the story.

6. Leave out the display for the others to view. (This is an especially nice project around open house or parent/teacher conference time.)

Teachers: Enlarge and send one of these slips home with nightly books to reinforce story structure skills.

Name _____ Date _____

Title and Author _____

Pages _____ Signature _____

The main character in the book is _____. Draw or describe this character.	**The setting for this book is _____. Draw or describe the setting (when and where the story happened).**

Name _____ Date _____

Title and Author _____

Pages _____ Signature _____

The story problem was	**Three events from the story are:**	**The problem was solved when**
	1.	
	2.	
	3.	

Teachers: Have fun practicing story structure skills with this game.

Story Quizzo

Type: a game to help the children focus on story structure and give them practice with asking questions

Materials: three books that are familiar to the class, and a set of question cards made up by either the teacher or the class

Set up: Tell the class they will play a quiz game like Jeopardy. Divide the children into three groups. Assign each group one of the books. Each group will work on making cards as follows:

- Write descriptions of the main characters.
- Describe the setting of the story.
- Tell about the main character's problem.
- Describe one of the events in the story.
- Tell how the problem was solved.

Procedures: 1. Divide the children into teams.

2. Choose one player from each team and read one of the cards out loud to them.

3. The players must listen to the clues, raise their hands, and answer by asking one of the following questions:

- Who is the main character in (state the name of the book)?
- What was one of the events that happened in (state the name of the book)?
- What was the setting of (state the name of the book)?
- How did (state the name of the book) end?
- What was the problem in (state the name of the book)?

4. The first person to raise his or her hand and ask the correct question will be awarded a point. The winning team will be the one with the most points.

Optional: The teacher can make up the cards.

> **Teachers:** The following pages will assist you in developing your students' sequencing skills. The ability to comprehend and follow sequence not only helps increase reading comprehension with stories and historical events, but can also aid the children with following sets of directions.

Helpful Tips:

Sequencing refers to the order of actions or events. Chronological order, which tells the order of events that have already occurred, can commonly be found in historical text. Other examples of sequence can be found in instructions or recipes.

Of all of the text structures, most children find sequencing the easiest to understand. This is probably because children see many examples of sequencing in their lives. They follow directions daily and often read and hear stories in which sequence plays a significant part.

Teaching children to identify signal words that often appear in texts containing sequence helps them learn to focus on the order of events. Some signal words are: *first*, *then*, *next*, *finally*, and *last*.

Teach sequence throughout the day. Children can be encouraged to recall the sequence of daily occurrences. For example, when the class returns from lunch, they can work together to recall the

steps taken before, during, and after lunch. (Washed hands, lined up, walked to cafeteria, got in the lunch line, etc.)

Children can also recall the sequence of events after reading or listening to a story. They can use their understanding of sequencing when planning stories or performing creative skits.

Strong sequencing skills will improve comprehension through improved recall. Sequencing will also help students follow specific directions and organize their writing with logically-ordered events.

Share with parents:
- Time Lines (p. 37)
- Book Mobile (p. 41)

Additional pages to reinforce sequencing:
- Story Element Science (p. 26)
- Writing Activity (p. 47)
- Causes and Effects in Pictures (p. 75)

Answer Key

Page 34

1. a. 5	b. 4	c. 3
d. 6	e. 2	f. 1

2. first, next, then, finally

Organize Sequence

Directions: Use these to help you with the sequence of events in a story. First read a story or paragraph. Write the title in one of the organizers. Then fill in the events.

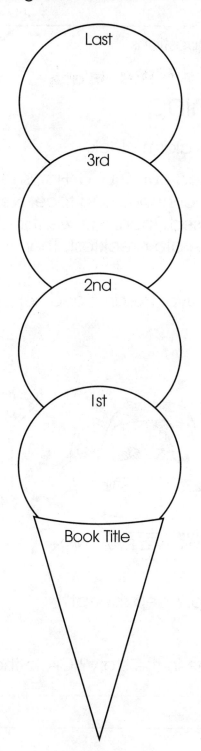

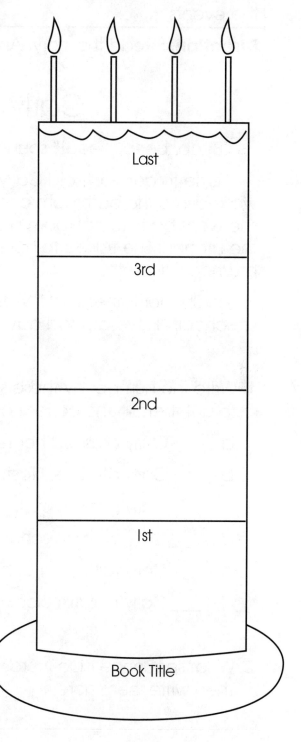

Practice Sequencing

Every story has a **sequence of events**. *Events* are the things that happen. *Sequence* is the correct order. Look for clue words such as **first**, **next**, **then**, and **last** or **finally**. They will help you sequence the events.

Directions: Read the story. Answer the questions.

Carly's Morning

"Beep, beep, beep!" sounded Carly's alarm clock.

"Time to get up," said Carly as she rolled out of bed. First, she walked into the bathroom and washed her hands and face. Next, she went back to her room and got dressed. Then, she went into the kitchen. She talked to her mom as she ate breakfast. Then, she brushed her teeth.

Finally, her father said it was time to leave. He dropped her off at school. "Have a good day," he said.

1. Write the number by these sentences to put them in the correct order.

   a. _____ Carly brushed her teeth.

   b. _____ Carly ate breakfast.

   c. _____ Carly got dressed.

   d. _____ Carly went to school.

   e. _____ Carly rolled out of bed.

   f. _____ Carly's alarm clock said, "Beep, beep, beep!"

2. What sequence clue words did you see in the story? Circle them. Then write them here. _____

_____

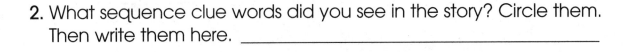

> **Teachers:** Practice sequencing skills with these journal prompts. Children will consider the concept of sequencing while writing. Enlarge and cut the prompts into cards for centers, use them on the overhead, or make a journal-prompt die.* Use the writing activity at the bottom of the page for more in-depth practice.

Journal Prompts

Sequencing	Sequencing	Sequencing
The first thing I do in the morning is _____ because ...	When I get home from school I do several things. First, I ... Next, I ... Finally, I ...	Explain how to make a bed. Make sure to put the steps in order! This is how I make my bed:
Sequencing	**Sequencing**	**Sequencing**
My favorite sandwich is a _____. This is how you make it:	The last thing I do when I get ready for bed is _____ because...	I like the book _____. Many things happened in this story. This is what happened:

*To make a die

1. Cut

2. Tape

3. Fold and tape

Name _____ Date _____

Writing Activity: This Is How

Directions: Think of something that you know how to do. Pretend you are teaching it to a friend.

I want to teach you how to _____.

These are the steps you follow:

1. _____

2. _____

3. _____

4. _____

Teachers: Enlarge and cut out these cards for use during math. They will strengthen sequencing and following-direction skills. They will also reinforce the steps taken while performing basic math tasks.

Direction Cards

ADDITION
1. Read the addition problem.
2. Hold up fingers to match the <u>second</u> number in the problem.
3. Say the <u>first</u> number in the problem and then <u>count on</u> with your fingers to find the sum.
4. The last number you say is the answer.

Three. 4, 5. The answer is 5.

MORE
1. Use counters and make sets equal to the two numbers.
2. Line up the two sets next to each other.
3. Make <u>pairs</u> using one item from each set.
4. The set that has some items <u>without</u> a pair is the set that has MORE.

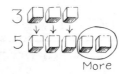

SUBTRACTION
1. Read the problem.
2. Hold up fingers to match the <u>first</u> number in the problem.
3. Look at the <u>second</u> number in the problem. Put that many fingers back down.
4. The number of fingers still up shows the answer.

Put up 3. Put down 2. The answer is 1.

LESS
1. Use counters and make sets equal to the two numbers.
2. Line up the two sets next to each other.
3. Make <u>pairs</u> using one item from each set.
4. The set that <u>doesn't have enough</u> to make pairs is the set that has LESS.

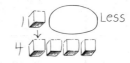

FINDING THE MISSING ADDEND
1. Read the problem.
2. Say the <u>number given</u> in the problem.
3. <u>Count on</u> until you reach the sum.
4. The number of fingers up is the answer.

Four. 5, 6, 7. The missing number is 3.

SAME
1. Use counters and make sets equal to the two numbers.
2. Line up the two sets next to each other.
3. Make <u>pairs</u> using one item from each set.
4. If each item has a pair, then the two sets have the SAME amount.

◎ **Comprehension**

Time Lines

Directions: Time lines are used in social studies. They show the sequence of things that happened. Make your own time line to show important dates in your life.

Think about your life. Choose the most important thing that happened to you during each year of your life.

When I was one_____.

When I was two_____.

When I was three _____.

When I was four _____.

When I was five _____.

When I was six _____.

Draw pictures on the time line to show these events.

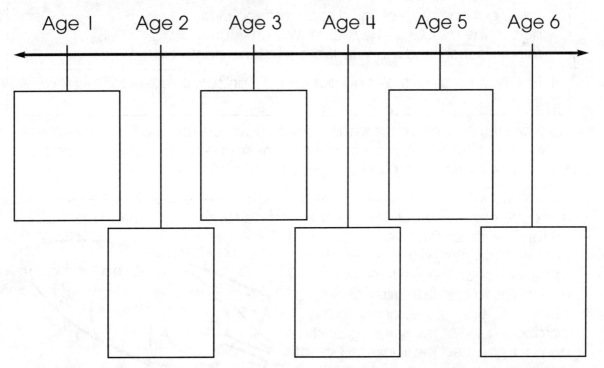

Compare your time line with others. How are they the same? How are they different?

Teachers: Following the correct sequence is very important in science experiments. Practice this comprehension skill whenever you experiment.

Follow the Steps!

Sample Experiment: Water Rockets

Materials: index cards, one shallow pan for each small group, liquid soap, crayons, and scissors

Preparation: On cardboard, make several stencils of the rocket prototype at the bottom of the page. Cut out rockets for children who are not able to cut.

Activity:

1. Explain that the class will be doing an experiment and that they need to remember the sequence of steps in the experiment.

2. Write the following on chart paper. Have children follow the steps:

> 1. First, make a rocket.
>
> 2. Next, lay the rocket on top of the water.
>
> 3. Then, put one drop of liquid soap into the circle hole in the middle of the rocket. Watch your rocket launch and shoot to the end of the pan!
>
> 4. Finally, rinse all of the soap out of the pan so it is ready for the next person.

3. After all of the children (or small groups) have performed the experiment, gather them together. Hide the directions and have the children recall the order of steps they used to perform the experiment.

4. Explain why the rocket shot across the water. The reason it did so is because soap molecules broke the surface tension by splitting up the water molecules that were lined up in a row and hanging on to each other. The soap caused the water molecules to spin like crazy and bump into each other and into the cardboard. All of this spinning and bumping caused the rocket to shoot across the water.

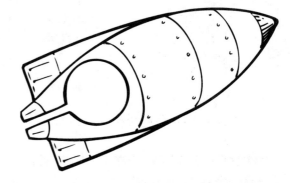

Comic Strips

Directions: Comic strips are a fun way to practice *sequence*. This comic strip is all mixed up! Cut apart the boxes. Look for sequence clue words like *first, next, last.* Put the boxes in the correct sequence. Now they tell a story!

Maybe a little less soap next time.

Then you put in some laundry soap.

It's easy! First you put in all the clothes.

Then you turn these dials until you hear the water. *Wow, that was easy.*

Let's help mom out. I know how to wash clothes. *Are you sure?*

> **Teachers:** Use this activity to reinforce sequencing skills during read-aloud time.

Balloon Toss

Materials: three to five balloons and a permanent marker

Preparation: Blow up the balloons and write one number on each, using the permanent marker.

Activity:

1. Read aloud any story, poem, or nonfiction reading selection.

2. Toss the balloons to the children listening. Have the children who catch the balloons line up in numerical order.

3. Finally, have the children retell the main events in order as follows:
   • The child with the number 1 balloon will tell the first event.
   • The child with the number 2 balloon will tell the second event.
   • Continue this way until the child with the number 5 balloon tells the final event.

Ideas for books that illustrate sequence:

The Little Old Lady Who Was Not Afraid of Anything by Linda Williams

Andrew's Loose Tooth by Robert N. Munsch

Alexander's Midnight Snack by Catherine Stock

A Tree for Me by Nancy Van Laan

Caps for Sale by Esphyr Slobodkina

The Grouchy Ladybug by Eric Carle

The Napping House by Audrey Wood

Teeny Tiny by Jill Bennet

This Is the Hat by Nancy Van Laan

Book Mobile

Directions: Follow the steps below to make a sequence book mobile.

Materials: hanger, yarn, hole punch, index cards, crayons, and markers

Steps:

1. Choose a book and read it.

2. Draw pictures of the main events on the index cards.

3. Put the pictures in order to tell the story.

4. Write the title on an index card.

5. Punch holes in the tops of the index cards.

6. Tie each card onto the hanger with the yarn. Make sure they are in the right sequence.

7. Hang up your mobile and enjoy it!

Teachers: Enlarge and send one of these slips home with nightly books to reinforce sequencing skills.

Name _____ Date _____

Title and Author _____

Pages _____ Signature _____

Write the three main events in this story.

1	
2	
3	

Name _____ Date _____

Title and Author _____

Pages _____ Signature _____

The story happened in this order:

In the beginning:	**In the middle:**	**At the end:**

Teachers: Have fun practicing sequencing skills with this game.

Order! Order in the Court!

Type: a fun game to help the children focus on sequence and give them practice with asking questions

Materials: rubber mallet, bathrobe, and desk or podium

Procedures:

1. Choose one child to be the judge. The judge will stand at the desk or podium and wear the robe. The judge will call out a sequence of 3 or 4 actions for the children in the "court" to perform.

2. After the children have performed the actions, the judge will pound the mallet and say "Order! Order in the court!" and then choose a new judge.

3. Once children have mastered remembering basic sequences, play "Order in the Court" with literature. In this version, the judge doesn't get to make up the sequence actions. The teacher holds up a book or says the name of a familiar story, and the judge has to recite a sequence of events from the story. The rest of the children then reenact these events, and the game continues like in #2.

Teachers: The following pages will assist you in developing students' prediction skills. Making predictions helps readers interact with the story before, during, and after reading.

Helpful Tips:

Prediction refers to making a guess about what the writer will write next. This guess is based on personal life experience and text clues. It doesn't matter if the prediction is correct or incorrect, because only the writer knows for sure what the reader is going to read next.

Most experienced readers enjoy thinking about what the writer is going to write next. When you have children make predictions about a book before it is read, you are helping them mentally prepare for reading. When you have the children make predictions while reading, you are helping them relate the text to their personal experiences, thus making it more meaningful and memorable. It also sets readers up to look for details that confirm their prediction, and makes them pay closer attention than if they had not made predictions.

Model this practice while you read aloud to your children. When you read a story about a child who is nervous, say, "I have been nervous before. This reminds me of the time that I… Everything turned out okay though. I think everything will turn out fine for the child in the book, too." Then continue reading. When everything does turn out fine, say, "See? My prediction was correct. I thought that would happen because I was fine, too!"

While you are reading ask the children to predict what they think will happen. Also, ask why they are making this prediction. Ask if it reminds them of something that happened before.

When children learn to relate the text to past experiences and interact with the author by making predictions, they will improve their comprehension and get more enjoyment from reading.

Share with parents:
- Writing Activity (p. 47)
- What's Behind the Door? (p. 53)

Additional pages to reinforce prediction:
- If I Had Been There… (p. 23)
- Making the Fastest Slide (p. 62)
- Drawing Conclusions from Art (p. 63)
- Magic Number Boxes (p. 72)
- What Caused This? (p. 79)

Organize Predictions

Directions: You can make predictions before, during, and after you read. Use these to help you. Choose one organizer. Write what you predict will happen. Then write the clues that back it up.

Practice Making Predictions

When you read, look for facts in words, titles, and pictures. Use these to **predict** what will happen next.

Directions: Make predictions as you read this story.

Look! A Martian!

1. Look at the title. What may happen in the story?

_____

"Look! A Martian!" yelled Quinn. The Martian walked right up to Quinn and said, "Eeep eeep-eeep."

2. Make a prediction. Do you think the Martian will be friendly? Why or why not?

_____

The Martian gave Quinn a lollipop. Then he smiled, showing little green teeth.

3. Was your prediction correct? What might happen next?

_____

"Hey, my dad is a dentist. Do you want him to look at your green teeth?" asked Quinn.

4. What do you think will happen next?

_____

5. On your own paper, write an ending for the story.

Teachers: Practice prediction skills with these journal prompts. Enlarge and cut them into cards for centers, use them on the overhead, or make a journal-prompt die.* Use the writing activity at the bottom of the page for more in-depth practice.

Journal Prompts

Prediction	Prediction	Prediction
Tim cut on foot. Predict what will happen next. Tell why you think so.	Jade is nervous. She is going to a new school. Predict how you think Jade's first day will go. Tell why you think so.	One time I was reading ____. I knew ____ was going to happen before I read it because …
Prediction	**Prediction**	**Prediction**
Tyler went outside to feed his dog. The dog ran very quickly to his bowl. Predict what will happen next. Give reasons why.	I predict the weather after school will be ____ because …	When I grow up, I predict I will be ____ because …

*To make a die

1. Cut

2. Tape

3. Fold and tape

Name _____ Date _____

Writing Activity: Guess What Happened!

Directions: Write a letter to a friend. Write about a funny thing that happened to you. Tell the first part, but leave off the ending. Ask your friend to guess what happened.

Dear _____,

Something funny happened to me. I was _____

_____

Can you guess what happened next?

Your friend, _____

 **Comprehension**

Making Predictions During Math

Materials: three different-sized jars filled with a variety of contents, crayons, small slips of paper (or copies of the forms below), and a box to keep the predictions

Preparation:

- Fill each jar with a set of small objects. (Example: Use an empty pickle jar and fill it with cotton balls, an empty baby food jar filled with small candy, or an empty peanut-butter jar filled with dried beans.)
- Label each jar with a number.
- Put the jars and the slips of paper in the math center.

Activity:

1. Remind the children that they have been learning how to make predictions. Tell them that they can make predictions in math, too.

2. Show the small slips of paper and the jars to the class. Suggest that they make a prediction about how many items are inside each jar. Prompt them to use clues to figure it out, rather than making a wild guess.

3. Store the jars and paper in the math center. Encourage the children to make predictions during the week and put them into the box.

4. At the end of the week, count the contents of each jar. Check to see whose predictions were the closest. Call on that student to share the clues he or she used to make the prediction. Award the winning child with the contents of the jar.

Name _____	Name _____
Date _____	Date _____
Predict how many items are inside the jar.	Predict how many items are inside the jar.
What clues did you use?	What clues did you use?
_____	_____
_____	_____

◎ **Comprehension** Prediction—Social Studies

Social Skills Prediction

Directions: Look at each picture. Make a prediction about what you think will happen next.

This picture reminds me of the time I

_____

What will happen next?

_____

_____

This picture reminds me of the time I

_____

What will happen next?

_____

_____

This picture reminds me of the time I

_____

What will happen next?

_____

_____

This picture reminds me of the time I

_____

What will happen next?

_____

_____

Teachers: Predictions are a basic element of science experiments. Point out the role prediction plays whenever you experiment. Draw parallels for your students between the way you use clues to make predictions in both science and reading.

Making a Hypothesis

Sample Experiment: Melting Ice

Materials: three ice cubes, three bowls, three small jars filled with one of the following: cold water, hot water, or salt

Activity:
1. Have the children tell what a prediction is. Tell them that a *hypothesis* is a prediction about what will happen during a science experiment.
2. Announce that they will be doing an experiment with ice cubes.
3. Show the children the three ice cubes. Tell them that you will poor cold water over one of the ice cubes, hot water over another ice cube, and salt over the third ice cube.
4. Say, "Now it is time to make science predictions, which are called *hypotheses.* Predict which ice cube will melt the quickest." Write the predictions on the board or on chart paper, on the left side of a chart.
5. Have the children help pour cold water over one of the ice cubes, hot water over another ice cube, and salt over the third ice cube.
6. Watch to see which ice cubes melt the quickest. Check which hypotheses or predictions were correct. Remind the children that when they are making predictions or hypotheses, it is okay to be incorrect, as long as the prediction was based on data.
7. Discuss how background knowledge can be useful in making predictions. Announce that you are going to perform the experiment again. Ask for predictions based on all the clues, including the new background knowledge. Record these on the right side of your chart, under the heading "New Predictions."
8. Perform the experiment again. Go back to the list of new predictions and check to see if these were more accurate. Ask students why their predictions were more accurate the second time. Use this opportunity to reinforce using all the background knowledge you have when making predictions.

	Predictions (Hypotheses)	New Predictions
Cold water:		
Hot water:		
Salt:		

How Will It End?

Directions: Look at the comic strip. It can tell you a story.
The last section is blank.

What do you predict will happen next?

_____

_____

What clues make you think that will happen?

_____

_____

Draw a picture that shows what you think will happen.

> **Teachers:** Use this activity to reinforce prediction skills during read-aloud time.

Ring the Prediction Bell

Materials: one bell (any sound maker can be used such as a whistle, a harmonica, or two blocks to hit together)

Activity:

1. Show the children the *prediction bell.* Tell them "When I am reading, I may stop and ring the *prediction bell.* When you hear the bell, think about what will happen next."

2. Read aloud any story, poem, or nonfiction reading selection.

3. Periodically, stop reading and ring the *prediction bell.* Then, have the children think quietly about what they think will happen next. Call on someone to share their prediction and the clues that led to that prediction.

4. Continue reading and then stop so that the children can check their predictions.

Optional: You may have the children discuss their predictions with each other before calling on some of them to share. This way, they will see that people often have different predictions, and it is okay if the predictions are incorrect as long as they are backed up by some kind of evidence.

Ideas for books that illustrate prediction:

A Tree for Me by Nancy Van Laan

Curious George at the Fire Station by Margret and H. A. Rey

Froggy Bakes a Cake by Jonathan London

How Is a Moose Like a Goose? by Robin Michal Koontz

Little Peep by Jack Kent

Wake Me in Spring by James Preller

Alexander, Who's Not (Do You Hear Me? I Mean It!) Going to Move
by Judith Viorst

What's Behind the Door?

Teachers: Make these "prediction doors" to help children practice prediction skills.

Materials: construction paper, markers or crayons, and scissors

Preparation:

- Copy and cut out one door and one larger construction-paper rectangle for each child.

- Glue the left-hand side of the door onto the rectangular paper. Fold the door open to dry.

Activity:

1. Have each child choose a favorite book or story to write about.

2. Tell them to think of the most exciting part of their stories. They will use this part of the story to test their friends' prediction skills.

3. Give each child a "prediction door." Demonstrate how to open and close it.

4. Have the children write part of the story on the outside of the door. The children who are not able to write can either draw a picture or dictate the story. Tell the children to stop writing at an exciting part.

5. Now, have the children open the door and write the next part of the story on the inside. (Again, the nonwriters will need some assistance.) Remind them to keep the writing and pictures behind the door so that when the door is closed, no one will be able to see.

6. One at a time, have each child show and read the outside of his or her door. The class can make predictions about what will be written behind the door. After the predictions have been made, let the speaker read and show what is behind the door!

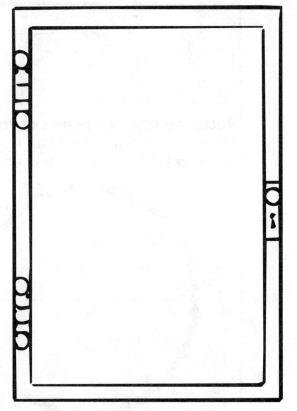

Comprehension

Teachers: Enlarge and send one of these slips home with nightly books to reinforce prediction skills.

Name _____ Date _____

Title and Author _____

Pages _____ Signature _____

Look at the cover and read the title of a new book. What do you think the book will be about? Write your prediction below. Then write the clues you used.

Prediction

Clue

Clue

Clue

Name _____ Date _____

Title and Author _____

Pages _____ Signature _____

Read the first two pages of your book. Stop reading and make a prediction about what will happen next. Write your prediction below. Then write the clues you used.

Clue

Clue

Prediction

When you finish reading, check:
Was your prediction correct?

yes   no

What's in the Bag?

Type:　　　　a game to help children develop clue-based prediction skills

Materials:　　pillowcase or bag, a set of small items (blocks, small stuffed animal, tape dispenser, book, and so on)

Procedures:　
1. Choose one child to reach his or her hand deep inside the bag. He or she will use hands and fingers to feel an item. Without looking, the child should try to figure out what the item is without saying anything.

2. Once the child has a good idea of what the item is, he or she will use three words or phrases to describe the item to the class.

3. The rest of the children try to predict what the child is holding based on the description. The first child to guess the item correctly can be the next person to choose and describe an item.

Whosiwhatsit?

Type:　　　　a guessing game to reinforce the importance of clues and prior experience in making predictions

Materials:　　rare or unusual objects that the class won't recognize

Procedures:　
1. Show the class the unusual object. Give them two or three minutes to look at it and silently think about what it may be. (You may or may not want to pass it around.)

2. Have students turn to someone near them and take turns sharing their predictions and the clues that make them think so.

3. Call on a few students to share with the class. Record one or two predictions in a graphic organizer to build the connection between clues and predictions. Finally, reveal the true identity and purpose of the object.

Optional:　　Instead of using objects, tie this game in with books by using the same process with something you see in an illustration. For vocabulary building, read a sentence with a mysterious word, and use the same process to guess its meaning from the context.

Teachers: Use the following pages to help you work on drawing conclusions with your class. Drawing conclusions involves a mental process where the children relate what they are reading to their own experiences, thus forming a deeper comprehension of the text.

Helpful Tips:

Drawing conclusions is all about "reading between the lines." The answers to some comprehension questions are "right there," directly stated in the text where children may look back and find them. Sometimes, though, answers are not directly stated in the text. This information is inferred. To answer these questions, children must draw conclusions. This challenges them to comprehend the text at a higher level.

Authors often let you draw your own conclusions about events or characters' actions. They may leave hints or clues for the reader to base conclusions on. At every opportunity, model noting these clues and using them to draw a conclusion.

Children draw conclusions and make inferences in their everyday lives. For example, if you ask children what they think may have happened to a crying child lying on the ground next to a bicycle, they may infer or draw the conclusion that the child fell off the bike. Although the children did not actually see or hear the event, they still are able to draw conclusions.

Model this strategy when you are reading aloud to the class. When Goldilocks is woken up by the bears and runs from the house say, "Goldilocks must have been very surprised and afraid when she woke up and saw the three bears staring down at her." Feelings that characters are experiencing are inferred. By modeling this behavior, you demonstrate how to have a deeper interaction with the text.

Share with parents:

• Drawing Conclusions from Art (p. 63)

Additional pages to reinforce drawing conclusions:

• Beach Ball Blast! (p. 28)
• What and Why? (p. 76)
• Good Soil Versus Bad Soil (p. 74)
• What's in the Bag? (p. 55)
• What Caused This? (p. 79)

Answer Key

Page 58
1. lemonade
2. She mixed together all the ingredients for lemonade: water, lemon juice, and sugar.
3. a

Page 60
1. The one on the right. The water level is higher.
2. The one on the left. The plate is fuller.
3. The one on the left. The boy has to work harder to carry it.
4. The one on the right. It's moving slower.

Page 61
1. 6
2. strawberry
3. apples
4.–6. Answers will vary.

◎ Comprehension

Organize Conclusions

Directions: Use these to help you draw conclusions. First read a story or paragraph. Think, "What conclusion can I draw from my reading?" Write your conclusion in one of the organizers. Then write the clues that support it.

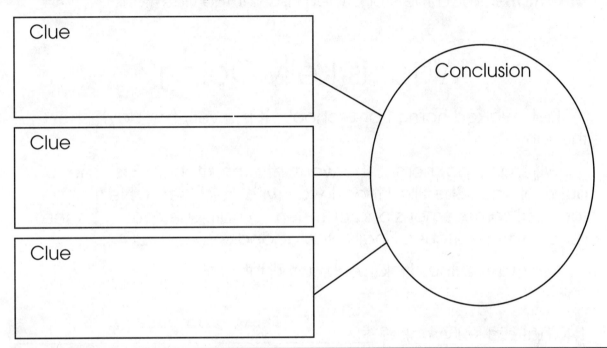

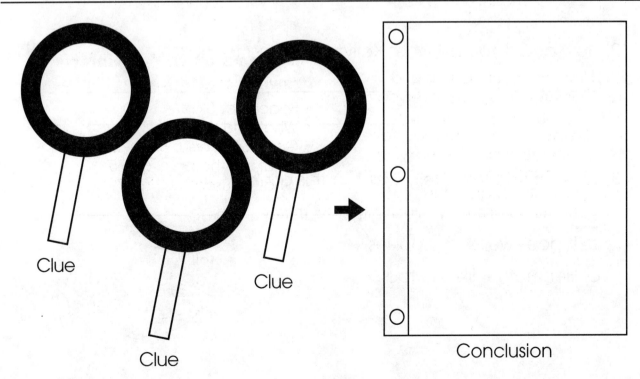

Practice Drawing Conclusions

Sometimes readers are like detectives. They use word and picture clues to **draw conclusions**. This helps them understand what is going on in a story or book.

Directions: Read the story. Then answer the questions.

What Is Kelly Doing?

Kelly walked home from school. "It is a very hot day," she thought.

When she got home, she went into the kitchen. First, she took out a pitcher. She filled it part way with cold water. Next, she took out some lemons and cut them in half. She squeezed the juice into the pitcher. Finally, she added some sugar.

Kelly tasted the drink. "Ahh, just right," she said.

1. What did Kelly make?_____

2. How could you tell what Kelly was going to make?

_____

_____

3. Why do you think Kelly wanted this drink?

   a. It was a hot day, and she was thirsty.

   b. It goes well with cookies.

   c. Her mother likes it, too.

Teachers: Practice drawing-conclusion skills with these journal prompts. Enlarge and cut them into cards for centers, use them on the overhead, or make a journal-prompt die.* Use the writing activity at the bottom of the page for more in-depth practice.

Journal Prompts

Conclusions	**Conclusions**	**Conclusions**
Mom went to the store. She got sauce, cheese, meat, and dough. What do you think she was going to make? Why?	The conclusion is that the boy loves school. Write three sentences that can make you think this without saying "the boy loves school."	The conclusion is that it is a rainy day. Describe what the sky, trees, and grass look like at the park.
Conclusions	**Conclusions**	**Conclusions**
Write a story that lets the reader know it is cold outside without using the words "It's cold outside."	When I read a story, I try to figure out what the author is trying to tell me by…	Draw a conclusion about how your teacher is feeling today. Describe the clues that make you think so.

*To make a die

1. Cut

2. Tape

3. Fold and tape

Name _____ Date _____

Writing Activity: What Do I Like to Do?

Directions: Write a letter to a friend. Think of something you like to do. Describe it to your friend, but don't say what it is. Your friend will have to draw his or her own conclusion.

Which Has More?

Directions: You can draw conclusions in math. Look for clues in each picture. Circle the one that has **more**. Then write the clues that made you think so.

1.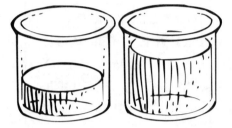

_____
_____
_____

2.

_____
_____
_____

3.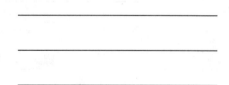

_____
_____
_____

4.

_____
_____
_____

Conclusions from Graphs

**Draw your own conclusions from looking at the graph.
Answer the questions below.**

Favorite Fruits	
banana 🍌	☺
apple 🍎	☺ ☺ ☺ ☺ ☺ ☺
strawberry 🍓	☺ ☺ ☺ ☺ ☺ ☺ ☺ ☺
watermelon 🍉	☺ ☺ ☺ ☺

 ☺ = 1 child

1. How many children liked apples? _____

2. Which fruit was the most popular? _____

3. If you offered apples and bananas to the children,
   which would you run out of first? _____

**Ask 5 friends which fruit they like best. Record their answers
on the graph.**

Favorite Fruits	
grape 🍇	
apple 🍎	

**Draw your own conclusions from looking at the graph.
Answer the questions.**

4. How many children liked grapes? _____

5. Which fruit was the most popular? _____

6. If you offered apples or grapes to the children, which would
   you run out of first? _____

_____

Teachers: At the end of nearly every experiment, the experimenters draw conclusions. Point this out to students during science. This is a great way to practice the skill of gathering clues and using them to formulate conclusions.

Making the Fastest Slide

Sample Experiment: Sliding Materials

Materials: four wooden rulers, wooden blocks, masking tape, four quarters, aluminum foil, waxed paper, sandpaper, and fabric

Activity:
1. Tell the children that they will be testing materials to see which makes the best slide for quarters.
2. Have the children look at the materials and make predictions about which would make the fastest slide. Write the predictions on the board or on chart paper.
3. Have the children build a base for the slide out of blocks (or books). Cover each of the rulers with one of the materials to be tested. Use the masking tape to secure the material to the back of each ruler. Take care not to have wrinkles in the material once it has been attached to the ruler.
4. Choose two volunteers to lay the quarters at the top of each slide (one quarter in each hand, so all four quarters can "race" at once). Make sure that the bottoms of the slides are even! (You may want to tape the back of the rulers to the table so they stay even.) Have the volunteers practice letting go of their quarters and letting them slide to the bottom of the slide.
5. Have the volunteers lay the quarters at the top of each slide again and let go of the quarters at the same time. Record which quarter reaches the bottom first. Do this three or four times to be sure of the results.

Conclusion:
Lead the class in a discussion about the results of the experiment. Have them answer the following questions:
- Which material makes the best sliding material?
- Which material makes the worst sliding material?
- Why do you think some materials are faster than others?

Drawing Conclusions from Art

Directions: Look at the picture. What may have happened? What is about to happen? Draw your own *conclusion*. Then write a story about the picture. (You may add other details to the picture to go with your story.)

_____

_____

_____

_____

_____

_____

_____

_____

_____

Finding the Hidden Message

Material: magnifying glass

Activity:

1. Show the children the magnifying glass. Tell them that when you are reading, you may stop and give someone the magnifying glass. Explain that the person who has the magnifying glass will have to draw a conclusion from the text or tell about the hidden message.

2. Read aloud any story, poem, or nonfiction reading selection.

3. Periodically, stop reading and give the magnifying glass to someone. Ask a question like, "How do you think the character is feeling?" "What do you think the character is thinking?" or "Do you think the character is happy about what happened? How can you tell?" After the child shares his or her conclusion, continue reading.

Optional: After the child has shared his or her prediction, have the rest of the class tell whether they have drawn the same conclusion or a different one.

Ideas for books that illustrate drawing conclusions:

Alligator Baby by Robert N. Munsch

Can I Have a Stegosaurus, Mom? Can I? Please!? by Lois G. Grambling

Can I Keep Him? by Steven Kellogg

Can You Guess Where We're Going? by Elvira Woodruff

Fish Is Fish by Leo Lionni

Hattie and the Fox by Mem Fox

Jerome Camps Out by Eileen Christelow

The Witch Next Door by Norman Bridwell

Learn a Lesson While Reading

Directions: Use this page to write a letter to an author. First, read a book. Then fill in the lines below. Tell the author what you learned from his or her book.

Dear Author,

I read your book called _____.

I learned a lesson from this book. The lesson I learned was _____

_____

_____

I learned this when the main character _____

_____

_____

This lesson will help me _____

_____

_____

I think this book is _____

Sincerely,

_____

Try this! Now you can cut out your letter and mail it!

 **Comprehension**

Teachers: Enlarge and send one of these slips home with nightly books to reinforce drawing-conclusion skills.

Name _____ Date _____

Title and Author _____

Pages _____ Signature _____

How was the character feeling during the story?

Circle or draw the character feeling this way.

Conclusion

How can you tell the character felt that way? List the clues.

Clues

Name _____ Date _____

Title and Author _____

Pages _____ Signature _____

During what season did the story take place?

Circle or draw it.

spring   summer   fall   winter

How can you tell?
List the clues.

Clues

_____

_____

_____

_____

Teachers: Have fun practicing drawing-conclusion skills with this game.

Conclusion Charades

Type: a game to help the children focus on story structure and give them practice with asking questions

Set up: Copy the game cards below and cut them apart.

Procedures:
1. Divide the children into small groups. Have each group select one of the cards to act out. Tell the children that the only time they can talk is when they are asking the question at the end of their skit. (The skit will be like charades.)

2. After the children have had time to rehearse, bring the class back together. Have the groups act out their skits, one at a time. The rest of the class will have to guess the conclusion.

- Children were swimming.
- Children were fanning themselves.
- Children were wiping sweat from their foreheads.

What time of year is it?

Conclusion: Summer

- You see a lot of dogs.
- You see a lot of cats.
- You see a vet.

Where are you?

Conclusion: You are at a vet's office.

- A person has a suitcase.
- The person sees another person and calls his or her name.
- The two people run to each other and hug.

What is happening?

Conclusion: The person has been on a trip or is visiting from out of town.

- Several children are fighting over a toy.

Why are the children upset?

Conclusion: The children wanted the same toy.

Teachers: The following pages will assist you in modeling and practicing cause and effect skills. Learning to see the relationships between events and actions leads to better comprehension in many curriculum areas.

Helpful Tips:

Cause and effect describes the relationship between two actions. Understanding cause and effect means understanding the "why" in relationships. Cause and effect writing is found in the science, history, and geography curriculums, as well as literature.

This skill has been deliberately addressed last in this book because all the prior skills addressed are prerequisites for understanding cause and effect.

Pointing out signal words that often show cause/effect relationships can help children learn to identify these relationships. Some of these signal words are: *because, therefore, since, as a result of,* and *so.*

There are many fiction books that are good examples of cause and effect relationships. (*If You Give a Mouse a Cookie, If You Give a Moose a Muffin, If You Give a Pig a Pancake,* all by Laura Joffe.

Choose one of these books to read to your class. Then ask cause questions such as, "Why did _____ happen?" or "What caused _____?" Also include effect questions such as, "What happened because _____?" or "What was the result of _____?"

Looking for the reason why things happen (cause/effect) is part of our human nature. Therefore, understanding the cause/effect text structure is essential in learning how our world works. In addition, being able to foresee results of actions and events can produce more responsible citizens.

Share with parents:

• Writing Activity (p. 71)

Additional pages to reinforce cause and effect:

• Follow the Steps! (p. 38)
• Drawing Conclusions from Art (p. 63)

Answer Key

Page 70

1. a
2. b
3. c

Organize Cause and Effect

Directions: Use these to help you with cause and effect. Write a cause in one of the organizers. Then write the effect after the cause that made it happen.

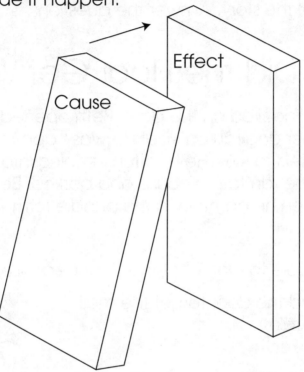

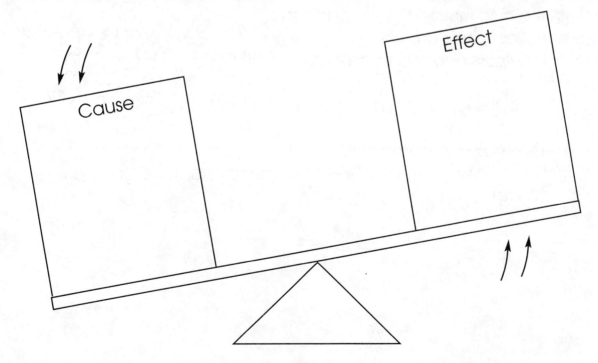

Practice Cause and Effect

An action can make something else happen. The action is a **cause**. What happens is the **effect**.

Directions: Read the story. Answer the questions.

How Did the Floor Get Wet?

The mailman knocked on the door. Beth opened it to get her mail. Just then, her dog ran outside! He was happy to play in the yard. Then it started to rain. He had fun jumping into the rain puddles. Finally, he ran to the house and barked. Beth opened the door for him. When he came in, a big puddle formed on the floor.

1. The dog was able to run out of the door because…

    a. Beth opened the door to get the mail.
    b. it started to rain.
    c. the dog barked.

2. Puddles formed on the ground because…
    a. the dog jumped in the puddles.
    b. it was raining.
    c. the grass needed to be cut.

3. What caused the big puddle on the floor?
    a. It was raining.
    b. The mailman came inside.
    c. The dog was dripping wet from the rain, and he got the floor all wet.

Teachers: Practice cause and effect skills with these journal prompts. Enlarge and cut them into cards for centers, use them on the overhead, or make a journal-prompt die.* Use the writing activity at the bottom of the page for more in-depth practice.

Journal Prompts

Cause	**Cause**	**Cause**
One morning I was very tired because…	The cat ran across the yard and up into a tree when…	I was not able to do my homework because…
Effect	**Effect**	**Effect**
Since it was raining outside…	Because I got a good grade on my test, Mom and Dad…	If everyone throws one piece of garbage on the floor, then…

*To make a die

1. Cut

2. Tape

3. Fold and tape

Writing Activity: If You Give a Bear a Book

Discuss how actions can cause a chain of events. Have the children work together to make a class book about a chain of events like Laura Joffe's *If You Give a Mouse a Cookie*.

1. Together as a class, brainstorm and record a chain of causes and effects, beginning with "If you give a bear a book, then you have to…"

2. Continue with the pattern "If you (effect from previous event), then you have to (new effect)." Let every child contribute one sentence, recording it on an overhead, board, or chart paper.

3. When you have one sentence per child, instruct students to copy the sentence they contributed onto their own paper. Then let them illustrate it. (You may create more than one sentence per child if students want to make multiple pages.)

4. Compile all the pages to create a class book. Have the children help make a cover for the book and title it "If You Give a Bear a Book."

Teachers: Make the following boxes to help children recognize and practice cause and effect relationships in math.

Magic Number Boxes

Materials: several cardboard jewelry boxes, index cards, resealable bags, and markers

Preparation:
- Cut the index cards into pieces that are about two-thirds the size of your boxes.
- Cut a slit in the bottom of each box, near one of the edges. Make sure the slit is big enough for the index card to easily slide through.
- Choose a number (this will be your magic number) to add to the target numbers that will be found on the index cards. Write "If I add 2" on the bottom of the box. (The number 2 can be replaced by any number.)
- Program the index cards with target numbers. Draw an arrow pointing up at the top of the target numbers so the children will know which side to look at when they slide the card into the box. On the back of each card write the sum that will be reached after the "magic number" is added.
- Store the "Magic Number Box" with its flash cards in a resealable bag.

Activity:
1. Have the child choose one of the index cards and look at the number that has an arrow above it.
2. Next, the child will look at the "magic number" on the bottom of the box and say, "If I add 2 then I will have…"
3. The child will slide the card into the box, arrow first.
4. Finally, the child will flip the box over, open it up, and see what number is showing now! If he or she was correct, this will be the sum that he or she predicted!

Responsibility

Activity:

1. Lead a class discussion about responsibility and citizenship. Copy this chart on the board or chart paper. Record the effect students share.

Cause	Effect
• If I do my homework…	
• If I do not do my homework…	
• If I put away my toys…	
• If I do not put away my toys…	
• If I listen while my teacher is talking…	
• If I do not listen while my teacher is talking…	
• If I share with my friends…	
• If I do not share with my friends…	

2. Discuss how "I will get in trouble" is not the main reason for doing what is right. For example, a child may suggest that "If I do not do my homework, I will not be able to play at recess." Explain that while this is definitely a consequence, a worse consequence would be that he or she would not be able to practice the skill that the teacher wants him or her to learn.

3. For further extension, have the children come up with their own sentence prompts.

Teachers: Cause and effect relationships are an essential part of science experimentation. After setting up and performing a science experiment, good scientists always make note of causes and effects.

Good Soil Versus Bad Soil

Sample Experiment: The Effects of Soil Quality

Materials: two small pots, seeds, good potting soil (purchased at a garden store), poor soil (soil with sand, rocks, or clay), water supply, and sunlight

Activity:
1. Have the children prepare two pots. One pot should contain good potting soil and the other should contain poor soil. Label each pot.
2. Have the children place two seeds in each pot.
3. Water the plants daily with the same amount of water. Put the plants outside so that they receive sunshine every day.
4. Check on the pots and record observations on the form below, if desired. After three weeks, draw conclusions.

Conclusion:
The children will notice that the seeds grown in the good potting soil are healthier. They can assume that the reason the plants in the good potting soil are healthier is because the good soil is better for the plants. Good soil has more of the nutrients plants need to be healthy and strong.

Name _____ Date _____

The Effects of Good and Bad Soil

Directions: Record your observations each week. At the end, write your conclusion about the effects of good and bad soil.

	Week 1	Week 2	Week 3	Conclusion
Plant in good soil				
Plant in bad soil				

Causes and Effects in Pictures

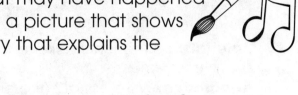

Directions: Look at the picture. What may have happened before this picture was taken? Draw a picture that shows what happened before. Write a story that explains the picture and what *caused* it.

What happened before?

_____

_____

_____

_____

_____

_____

_____

_____

_____

_____

> **Teachers:** Use this activity to reinforce cause-and-effect skills during read-aloud time.

What and Why?

Materials: permanent marker and two soft balls

Preparation: Write "What? (the effect)" on one ball and "Why? (the cause)" on the other ball.

Activity:

1. Read a story or poem to the children.

2. Stop reading and toss the balls to two students. Have the child who catches the "What?" ball tell what just happened. Have the child who catches the "Why?" ball tell what caused this to happen.

3. Continue reading, stopping, and tossing the balls until the end of the story or poem.

Ideas for books that illustrate cause and effect:

If You Give a Moose a Muffin by Laura Joffe Numeroff

If You Give a Mouse a Cookie by Laura Joffe Numeroff

If You Give a Pig a Pancake by Laura Joffe Numeroff

Library Lil by Suzanne Williams

The Rainbow Fish by Marcus Pfister

The Patchwork Farmer by Craig Brown

◎ Comprehension

Acting Out Causes and Effects

Directions: Read a book. Then fill in the lines below. Use this paper to help you make a skit about your book.

1. **Effect:** Something that happened in the story was _____

    _____

    _____

2. **Cause:** This happened because _____

    _____

    _____

Now make up a skit or play. It should show the story event you just wrote about.

3. What characters do you need?_____

    _____

4. Do the characters say any lines? Write them here:

    _____

    _____

    _____

    _____

    _____

    _____

5. Choose people to help you act out the skit. Then perform it. If you have lines, read them off the page. Have your friends tell you what cause and effect you acted out.

Teachers: Enlarge and send one of these slips home with nightly books to reinforce cause and effect skills.

Name _____ Date _____

Title and Author _____

Pages _____ Signature _____

Tell about something that happened in the story.

Why did this happen?

Effect

Cause

Name _____ Date _____

Title and Author _____

Pages _____ Signature _____

One thing the character did in the story was

The character did this because

Effect

Cause

Teachers: Have fun practicing cause and effect skills with these games.

Dominos and Mousetrap

Type: well-known games that help children recognize chains of causes and effects

Materials: a Mousetrap game, dominos

Procedures: There are several games that can help children understand cause and effect relationships. *Mousetrap*, the board game, can be used as a good visual example of cause and effect and chain events. Turning the crank starts a chain of events that eventually help to trap a mouse. Have the children work together to set up the trap. Then the children can take turns trapping the mouse.

Dominos are also a good game that can illustrate cause and effect and a chain of events. Have the children work together to line up the dominos. After the first domino is knocked over, it starts a chain of events that is only completed when the last domino has fallen.

What Caused This?

Type: a guessing game to build the skills of cause and effect as well as drawing conclusions about text from word or picture clues

Materials: books which are unfamiliar to the class

Set up: mark pages in books with interesting causes and effects

Procedures: Show or read students a page or passage that shows an interesting effect. Have students think about what could have caused it, then tell their ideas to someone near them. Finally, call on some students to share their answers with the class, giving evidence for their predicted cause. Flip back the page or read the previous passage to reveal the answer to the class. Continue in this way for as long as you want to play.

Optional: Switch up the game and tie it in with prediction by playing "What's the Effect." This is played the same way, just in reverse: Show the cause and have students try to predict the effect.

Think Like a reader!

I am reading _____

Why did I choose this book?   ☐ Fun!   ☐ To learn something new.

What do I think the book is going to be about?

☐ **This book is pretend.**

While I read, I will remember:

• Characters

• Setting

• Plot

Here is a picture of my favorite part:

Would I give this book to a friend?   ☐ Yes   ☐ No

☐ **This book is real.**

What do I think the book is about?

While I read, I will remember:

• Facts

• Things I think are interesting:

Here is a picture of something I learned:

Would I give this book to a friend?   ☐ Yes   ☐ No